The Alchemical Keys to Masonic Ritual

By Timothy W. Hogan

PM, 32* KCCH, KT, ROS, FRC, S.I.I. PSM of AMD

Copyrighted © 2007

ISBN: 978-1-4357-0440-4

Acknowledgements

Special Thanks goes to East Denver Lodge #160, AF&AM, the Denver Consistory of the Scottish Rite, the Knights of St. Andrews, the Scottish Rite Research Society, Denver Chapter #2 Royal Arch Masons, Denver Council #1 Cryptic Masons, Denver-Colorado Commandery #1 Knights Templar, the Colorado College of Masonic Societas Rosicruciana In Civitibus Foederatis, East Denver AMD Council # 425, The Grand College of Rites- USA, the Royal Order of Scotland, Enlightenment Lodge, The Templar Research Institute, Research Lodge of Colorado, the Grand Lodge of Colorado, the Grand Lodge of New Mexico, and the Grand Lodge of France.

I also want to give a special thank you to the following brothers for their help and support over the years: J. Freed, H. Zoufalli, B. Lasater, E.B. Jackson, N. North, B. Rux, L. Frazier, T. Hornsby, C. Porter, R. Bernard, G. Ford, W. Arner, R. Mahoney, R. Birely, D. Cline, D. Wolenhopt, T. Kissam, D. Calloway, A. Kampolt, H. Warren, H. Hogan, G. Teter, C. Weston, J. Hopkins, W. Glover, D. Schweitzer, D. Day, G. Bevel, R. Weingarten, J. Mack, A. Cooley, R. K. Milheim, D. Tygart, M. Hessel, D. Sayoun, B. House, G. Sardenson, K. Shepherd, C. Stuetheit, and R. Smith.

The Alchemical Keys to Masonic Ritual

Introduction

I come from a long line of Freemasons- going back to General Joseph Warren of the Revolutionary War and further, and many of the keys to Masonic ritual are such that they are passed on from mouth to ear, from generation to generation. These ideas have then been propagated in lodges in the past, for new brothers to gain the light which has been preserved for generations. Over the last century, there are many elements of Freemasonry that have become lost to many lodges which have perpetuated the work, and as a result, some of the secrets of Freemasonry have not been perpetuated. It is shocking, therefore, to hear brothers say that the only secrets to Freemasonry are the grips and passwords, as it is clear to "those who know" that these grips and passwords are merely the keys to the secrets of Freemasonry, and not the actual secrets themselves. Behind every symbol in Freemasonry are multiple levels of meaning, and it has always been the desire of the Masonic institution that as a brother expands his knowledge, these other meanings will become apparent. Witnessing the conferral of a degree many times, doing the memory work, and meditating on the significance of what is being presented, can all lead to an awakening in Masonic Light.

Over the last ten years I have been asked by many lodges, in many states, and various countries, to give lectures on some of the hidden meanings behind these symbols. Inevitably, I am also asked about how they can purchase my book on this topic, which, until now, has not been available. This book therefore is an attempt to pass on some of these secrets to those who have been initiated, passed, and raised in the tradition. Since this book is meant to only be read by Freemasons themselves, I have endeavored to allude to many items out of ritual that only brothers within the tradition will be able to recognize. Therefore I may make mention of a second degree password without actually saying what that pass word is, so that those who are Masons will know what I'm talking about, and those who are not, will not understand. Therefore if you are not a Mason, and you are trying to read this, you may as well put the book down, as there are large sections that will just not make sense. If you truly want to know the secrets of Freemasonry, there is only one way to experience it, and that is to become one. Only by going through the initiatory work can all aspects of this information prove of any value in the transformation of your life, and those around you. For those of you who are brothers, I encourage you to read with an open mind, and review the degrees you have been through while reading this. I promise that it will provide further light on your quest, and you will be shocked to see that some of the very teachings of the craft itself have become the stone which the builders rejected.

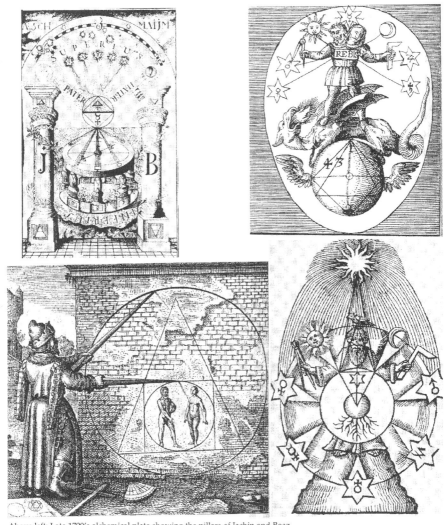

Above left: Late 1700's alchemical plate showing the pillars of Jachin and Boaz.
Above Right: Alchemical plate of 1625, by Heinrich Jamsthaler showing a figure with a square and compass. (Bottom right shows a similar one by Lazarus Zetzner of 1661).
Bottom Left: "The production of the Philosopher's Stone," by Michael Maier of 1618. Notice again the compass in his hands and square at his feet. In his alchemical text Maier states, "Make of man and woman a circle, from that a square, then a triangle, and then another circle, and you will have the philosopher's stone."

Chapter 1: Alchemy and Masonry?

When a candidate for Masonry goes through all of the various rituals of the many degrees composing the corpus of Freemasonry, they are confronted with many signs, symbols, gestures, and unalterable traditions which may at first seem foreign. It is the hope of the Masonic institution that, as the candidate progresses in degree work over the years and participates in the conferring of degrees, that he will come to understand the moral and esoteric implications of Masonic symbolism and will incorporate this new light into his life. Sadly, however, many of the origins of these symbols have been lost, and are now in hot debate by Masonic historians. As a result, the rituals are performed without most members understanding the full significance of what 'light' is being conferred. I hope to show through this book that some of the origins of Masonic ritual go back to alchemical terminology and craftsmanship, and allude not only to the transmutation of base metals into gold and elixir of life, but to the higher purpose of the transmutation of human character from a 'baser' to a more noble and golden state. I hope to show that all the signs, symbols, lectures, and titles of the Masonic ritual owe their origin to the alchemical tradition, and that through a better understanding of these alchemical keys, a new science is open to the Master Craftsman which can operate on the physical, mental, and spiritual levels of man's being. Fully expecting this hypothesis to be completely foreign to the average brother, I ask that all judgment be reserved until the case is completely presented.

The process and science of alchemy is a very arcane and difficult subject to present with people who are unfamiliar with it; in fact, it is even difficult to discuss with those who have studied it for years. I will . therefore try to be a thorough as possible. The word "alchemy" is generally believed to come from "al-khem" or "from the land of Khem"- which was Egypt. Even though most people associate alchemy with crazed magicians ingesting mercury and working in toxic fumes during the Middle Ages, the science of alchemy is actually quite ancient. Not only is it found in some of the oldest Egyptian texts, but we find it in the oldest Sumerian texts as well. In fact, the alchemical science in Sumer was called "GRA.AL", and this is almost unquestionably the origin of the Holy Graal- or "Grail" tradition. (This ancient history is covered extensively in the book *Revelation of the Holy Grail* by Chevalier Emerys). Alchemy was then fundamental to the institutions and philosophical schools of ancient Greece, and its doctrines were passed on by philosophers like Pythagoras, Plato, Socrates, and Aristotle. It was later propagated by the Essenes, early Muslims, Jewish Qabbalists, and the Knights Templar and cathedral builders in Europe. Finally, we also see it as the corner stone in the works of people like Francis Bacon, Isaac Newton, Robert Boyle, Elias Ashmole, and others who developed the Royal Society of Britain. Freemasons like Benjamin Franklin and Voltaire in the Lodge of Nine Muses studied alchemy in relation to Freemasonry, and several Masons were also known alchemists like the Comte de St. Germaine, Cagliostro, General Joseph Warren, Paul Revere, Dr. Benjamin Rush, and Thomas Jefferson. (Some would dispute Jefferson's involvement in Freemasonry since initiation records no longer survive for him, however the record of him being present at several public Masonic events and the fact that a Masonic code cipher was found among his personal papers should attest to the fact that he had more than just a side interest in the fraternity). Franklin wrote in his *Poor Richard's Almanack* of July 7th, 1757: "Get what you can, and what you get hold. 'Tis the Stone that will turn all your Lead into Gold." Albert Pike also believed that alchemy was THE great secret behind Freemasonry. All of these traditions had their part in the formation of Freemasonry, as will be found in many of the excellent books on the history of Freemasonry.

In a nutshell, alchemy can be defined as the process of taking something of a 'lower' or 'lesser' valued nature, and transmuting it into something of a 'greater' or 'more valuable' nature. This process is always done through the action of heat or fire. On a physical level, it has been compared to turning lead into gold. On the moral level in Masonic symbolism, it may be compared with turning the rough ashlar into the perfect ashlar through the heat produced by the action of the gavel of will. Psychologist Carl Jung equated it with turning from a will-less person to a self actualized individual, through the action of the 'heat' of daily trials and tribulations. On a spiritual level, it relates to the individual coming to a closer understanding and connection with their God through right moral action, prayer, and meditation during times of hardship. All of these describe the alchemical definition, but in order to understand how directly it relates to Freemasonry, I will need to describe the alchemical symbolism and the process of making the famed 'Philosopher's Stone"- or the Grand Arcanum of alchemy which turns base metals into gold, prolongs life, and stimulates consciousness.

Chapter 2: The Alchemical Process

The first stage in the alchemical literature for the production of the Philosopher's Stone, is for the Master Craftsman (alchemist) to choose an herb with a particular affinity for what was believed to be a planetary influence. The ancient alchemists recognized seven 'planets' made up of the Sun, Moon, Venus, Mars, Jupiter, Mercury, and Saturn. Each of these seven 'planets' ruled a respective day of the week, and our names of the days come from the Norse names for these planets; for example 'sun-day' and 'moon-day', "Tiw's day" (Tuesday and Mars), "Wotan's day" (Wednesday and Mercury), "Thor's day" (Thursday and Jupiter), and "Freya's day" (Friday and Venus). This planetary influence was believed to have corresponding associations in the body of the person, and by choosing and herb under the influence of, for example the sun, it was believed that the sun ruled the heart, and therefore that herb could help heal a weak heart if a medicine was made of it on Sunday. As exact knowledge of the heavens above and the earth below was therefore needed to make correlations. Already the globes on the pillars come into perspective. The Master Craftsman also needed to know the seven liberal arts and sciences to perform this function, and it should not be surprising that in the ancient world, each of the seven liberal arts and sciences was ruled by one of the seven planets.

After having found the herb needed, it was then pulled out of the ground by its roots, ground up as fine as possible with all parts in tact, and put in a vessel with either dew collected in the morning or rectified spirits of wine. (The dew allowed oils to separate from the herb and these oils could be easily separated from the water, and the spirits of wine absorbed the oils and collected them that way). After the herb was ground up and had the liquid placed at a low water mark above it, it was caused to sit and digest for twenty four hours- during which time it was shaken vigorously twice to help separate oils from the main body of matter in the vessel. As the green herb turned black, it was called by alchemists "caput mortum", which in Latin means "dead head". This was the first stage of the alchemical process. It was then distilled seven times, a process which turned the liquid reddish and then into a vaporous air, and then caused it to fall in a purified form as a whitish or clear fluid substance. This separated the components of the herb- with the body of the herb remaining behind in one vessel, and the vital components of the herb, containing the oils of it, being separated into another vessel. At the end of each distillation, oils from the herb were collected and were symbolically called the "sulphur" of the herb. The remaining liquid component the herb was originally sitting in was said to contain the symbolic "mercury"- or life force that was believed to come out of the air and be drawn into liquids like alcohol. The herb itself was said to have within it a special incorruptible body which was symbolically called the "salt" of the herb. At the end of the seventh distillation, the oils and the other liquid were put in one vessel, and the remaining herb was put into another. The combined oil and liquid was then sometimes called "heavenly dew" in alchemical language. The final remaining herb body at the end of this final stage was now no longer called "caput mortum", or "dead head", but rather became known as "feces", probably due to the fact that it had been completely digested in the vessel and now smelled with offensive effluvia! The final digestion occurred at the "bowels" of the vessel as all the liquid distilled away.

The next step in the process involved taking the remaining herb with oils distilled out of it, or "feces", and burning them to ashes in a calcination dish or crucible. The ashes would at first turn black, but as more heat was added to the ashes along with circulating air, the ashes would turn reddish in color. Symbolically all of these processes culminated in the symbolic killing of the herb. Next, the Master Craftsman would take the reddish ashes (called salts), and would subject them to a special corrosive process with heat and the use of strong alkalis and acids which would make the red salts turn into a bright white color. This white substance in alchemical terminology was called the 'secret salt', the 'spiritualized salt', the 'raised salt', and the 'hidden manna'. It was secret salt because only the Master Craftsman would be able to look for it and find it, whereas others would throw it away- not knowing what they had. Thus it was called the "stone that the builders rejected". This raised salt was said to be the key ingredient to bring the refined essence of the herb back to life. It was believed to be hidden in everything, and was thought to be of a special metallic nature- the seed of metals, though most people did not know how to look for it and therefore rejected it. Some of the largest concentrations of it were to be found in gold, grapes, pine, and wheat or corn. When Moses 'burned' the golden calf into a 'white powder', the alchemists recognized it as a code for this substance. In fact, it was believed that anytime the Bible alludes to 'white stone', 'manna', 'bread', or 'salt' that it was a code for this substance. The alchemists believed that Moses learned this technique from the Egyptians, as confirmed by the ancient historians Manetho and Flavius Josephus. The Egyptians described this substance in their texts like the Egyptian Book of the Dead, (also known as the Egyptian Book of Coming Into Light) as a white powder which they termed as a question- "what is it?" "Manna" in Hebrew likewise means- "what is it?" In their hieroglyphics, the Egyptians showed it as a loaf of bread. Further, in the Book of Jasher, one of the books removed from the Old Testament by early Jewish priests, it was Jethro the metallurgist who gave Moses the Ten Commandments of Yahweh, and not Yahweh himself! The alchemists believed that King Solomon knew the secret art of extracting this manna out of gold, which is why the Bible says that Solomon received 666 talents of gold each year in exchange for 'bread', and manna was also stored in the Ark at his temple.

This same 'manna' in Hebrew can be found in the old Sumerian texts as "she-manna", in the ancient Vedic texts as "vi-manna", in ancient Polynesian cultures as "manna", and in Tibetan and Cathar texts as "manni". It may have also been the inspiration behind the esoteric name of the founder of the Gnostic Christian Manichean sect, who went by "Manni" or "Mannes", and it is also behind the name of the Manadean Gnostic Christian sect- also called "John Christians" by the west. . It was further believed that when the Essenes referred to the "Semen of God" and "Teacher of Righteousness" in the Dead Sea Scrolls and other texts that it was alluding to this secret salt substance. Since this manna or secret salt behaved in ways that made it somewhat undetectable through normal means, this is why it was called the "stone that the builders rejected" and described as "what is it"- "manna?"

The medieval alchemists also believed that Jesus was an alchemist, as what is usually translated as "carpenter" in English, really comes from the more correct Greek translation (tekton) meaning "Master Craftsman"- which in Greek was a metallurgist and not a carpenter.

This is also why three wise Magi brought him gold, frankincense, and myrrh; as gold and pine resin (frankincense) are very rich in the secret salt, and myrrh was a meditative sedative. This is also why the Egyptian Pharaohs were buried with these three items. Symbolically, this is also why Jesus was said to be born from Mary, whose name means "salt water" or "sea", and he was born in Bethlehem- which means in Hebrew "House of Bread". If you remove the "t" or cross from "Christos"- the Greek word for "Christ", you get "Chrisos"- which is the Greek word for gold.

The final stage of the whole process was to take this white powder manna or secret salt and do a special process to it called "raising it", which would at first turn it black, and then it would turn blood red, and this new substance was called the 'red lion' or in some old texts as the "red dragon". This red powder (or salts) could be recombined with the saved oil (sulphur) and liquid (mercury) 'dew', and this final red elixir was known as the 'elixir of life'. This elixir of life was thought to be able to heal any part of the body and extend life spans, and was associated with the "holy grail". It was supposed to also taste like blood, and was sometimes called the "Blood of Osiris" in ancient Egyptian texts, and later it was called the "Blood of Christ" by Christian alchemists. By further taking this red liquid and doing a special process to it, it would turn white one last time, and this new white substance was said to transmute base metals into gold when heated. This last white phase was sometimes called the "white eagle".

The alchemists believed that the white manna, or "bread", and the red elixir, or "blood", were given to the twelve disciples by Jesus at the last communion, just as Moses baked manna into the shu-bread to feed the wandering Hebrews. They also believed that Jesus learned it from John the Baptist and the secret was passed to John the Evangelist- and this is why John the Baptist symbolically had his head cut off (caput mortum), and John the Evangelist wrote that "to he that overcomes will be given the hidden manna and the white stone". Perhaps this is also why the crucifixion takes place a Golgotha- a name meaning "skull"- or "dead head", which related to the beginning of the work out of which the Christos is removed from the cross or (t) – (tau), thus giving us "Chrisos"- meaning "gold".

In brief, this was the entire alchemical process. The only other key symbols in alchemy which related to this process consisted of the four elements of earth, water, air, and fire (and sometimes a fifth element called ether); the three principles of nature that needed to be combined to form the Philosopher's Stone, which were the sulphur, salt, and mercury; the two main planetary bodies (and polarities) found in ancient Hermetic writings of the sun and moon; and finally, the use of acids and alkalis in balance. The alchemists also adopted the qabbalistic sciences of the Hebrews in their terminology, and used the two main pillars from their qabbalistic diagrams to describe how all the components in the alchemical work went together. They also fervently wrote that unless one learns to transmute themselves into a better and more moral person while working the chemical process, then they will not succeed in the alchemical work. Also, the alchemists insisted that you could only crack their codes and be able to achieve the Red Lion with help from God. As the individual calcinated his bad habits, fears, and prejudices, he would then be able to produce the Grand Arcanum in the lab- also called the "Great Art". Symbolically then, the alchemists showed man composed of three main alchemical parts- composed of the sulphur or fire of the head, the mercury or air of the chest, and the salt or water of the abdomen.

Chapter 3: The Masonic Connection

Now, you may be saying that this is all very interesting and cryptic, but what does it have to do with Freemasonry? I will now go through Masonic ritual and show how it alludes directly to the alchemical process, and will then attempt to show how this could have been historically incorporated.

Alchemy first and foremost sought to join the physical with the spiritual. In alchemical symbolism, the physical world was represented by the square (like the four corners of the earth), and the spiritual world by a circle- which had no beginning or end. The two tools used in making these symbols are the square and compasses, and in the three degrees of symbolic blue lodge Masonry, the spiritual compasses gradually overcome the physical square as the candidate receives further light. In fact, early alchemical texts from the 1500's flatly state that in order to attain the famed Philosopher's Stone of alchemy, you needed to "square the circle". This is also why Leonardo Da'Vinci depicts a square and a circle joined around man in his Vitruvian Man drawing- with the square of earth centered on the genitals and the circle of spirit centered on the belly button. The abdomen between the two separates the higher and lower nature- which we can appreciate with the Mater Mason penal sign. Also, let us not forget- what is a square? It is an angle of 90 degrees, or the fourth part of a circle.

What might designated as the "blueprint" in blue lodge Masonry, is none other than the two pillars of the temple with the central pillar of man standing between them. As the brother moving through the EA degree becomes exposed to the left hand pillar of B:., the events in the ritual help him to understand that this pillar alludes to the left hand side of his body. Likewise, the FC Degree teaches the same correlation with the pillar of J:. and the right hand side of the body. Then by the MM degree, the brother has both pillars and is balanced, and has what in qabalistic diagrams has been called the 'tree of life', or 'Jacob's Ladder'. This diagram is made up of three pillars, three main levels or steps going up the pillars- demonstrated by the penal signs, ten spheres and 22 paths between the 10 spheres. The 10 spheres added to the 22 paths give us a total number of 32 combinations- and relates to the Scottish Rite degrees. Albert Pike gives this diagram and talks about it extensively in Morals and Dogma. In coming to understand this blue print as both a representation of the body and framework for consciousness, and an alchemical layout for the components of the alchemical work, the Philosopher's Stone, or Red Lion was deemed possible to be achieved. For example, it was believed that the top three spheres, or sephiroth on this qabbalistic diagram represented the establishment of the trinity of opposite forces, and the bottom seven spheres corresponded to the seven planets and/or metals, and days of creation. (Incidentally, the triangle formed by this trinity was sometimes depicted as an eye in a triangle- a symbol found in the east of many lodges in France, and later put on the Great Seal of the United States). The middle pillar of the tree was composed of the moon, mercury, and the sun in early alchemical texts- which we may recognize as the lesser lights- or sun, moon, and Master of the Lodge from the EA:. proficiency examination. (See the Tree Diagram on next page from Anton Kircher's Edipus Egyptiacus).

REPRESENTATION CONTAINING THE SUM TOTAL OF THE CABALA FOR INSERTION IN VOL. II, BOOK IV, CONCERNING CABALA OF THE HEBREWS

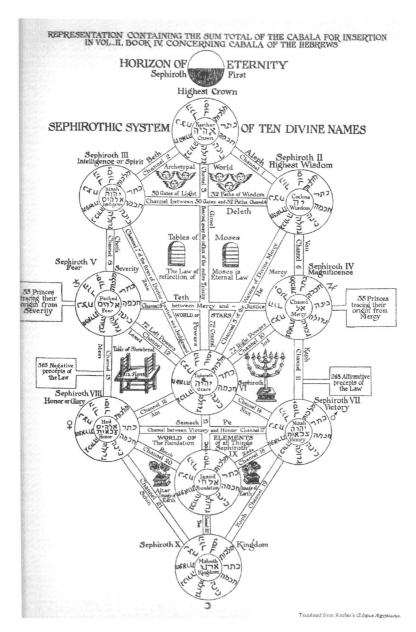

Now, in relation to alchemy it will be remembered from Masonic ritual that we learn to take the 'rough' ashlar and form it into the 'perfect' ashlar. This perfect ashlar of EA instruction is related to the EA himself- who is placed in the north east corner- like a corner stone of a building, which is at the point from coming out of the darkness of the north and into the first light of the east. This perfect ashlar then is the corner stone of all noble edifices. We also learn from FC instruction and corner stone ceremonies of the corn, wine, and oil, or Masonic wages, which in traditional alchemical symbolism and texts were said to be associated with salt, mercury, and sulphur respectively; (corn represented the body, or salt of the herb, wine carried the symbolic mercury or spirits, and the sulphur of an herb was its oil). These are sprinkled on a corner stone just as the compiling of the three principles of salt, sulphur, and mercury into a stone was said to be the creation of the Philosopher's Stone of alchemy.

Further, the Master Mason's apron is a square with an inverted triangle in it. This just happens to be the ancient alchemical symbol for a crucible or calcination dish, as found in the alchemical cipher keys of Valentinus from 1659 and in the keys of other alchemists of the period. Above the apron, the brother demonstrates the penal signs, which divide the body into the three main parts of fire (MM), air (FC), and water (EA)- as outlined by the penalties of each obligation in these three degrees. Also, remember from EA ritual that, "the earth alone of all the elements has never been found unfriendly to man". It is the action of fire, air, and water on earth that makes the Philosopher's stone. This relates to the very name 'Hiram Abiff', or "ChRM" Abiff in Hebrew. Fire, in Hebrew, is called ChAMAH, and relates to the head. Air in Hebrew, is called "RUACh", and relates to the chest. Water in Hebrew is "MAYIM", and relates to the abdomen. The first Hebrew letter of each of these words spells the name "ChRM"- or "Hiram". In Masonic ritual this is Hiram "Abiff"- coming from the old French 'biffet"- meaning "to eliminate" or "eliminated". "Hiram Abiff" means "Hiram the eliminated". It is the fire, air, and water that need to be rediscovered in the alchemical process in order to 'raise' the dead earth- or transmute matter from its dead to its alive and spiritualized state. These four elements can also be seen depicted in the four cardinal virtues. It should also be noted that the Hiram associated with King Solomon's temple in the Bible is renowned and called for by King Solomon because of his extensive knowledge in metals and metallurgy, and not necessarily for architecture. See the first Book of Kings 7:13,14; and the second Book of Chronicles (2:13-14).

The keys to rediscovering the parts of Hiram Abiff are within the three degrees themselves, and they outline the alchemical process. First of all, the EA degree's penal sign alludes to the caput mortum- or "dead head" stage of alchemy, or the herb being worked on. The tongue being buried in the 'rsotsalwmwtteafti24h'- alludes to the stage of 24 hours at the beginning of the work, and the need to shake the vessel twice in 24 hours, very vigorously, to help separate the oils from the herb. Also, alchemical texts are explicit about the fact that all herbs for the work need to be collected *by their roots* in order to obtain all the essence of the plant. Alchemical texts are also very clear that at this stage of the process, the herb is not to come in contact with metal of any kind- especially iron (a metal which contaminates other metals easily), which relates to the divesting of all metallic substances at the beginning of the EA degree and to the emphasis that no tool of iron was used at the construction of King Solomon's temple. (Iron was also related to Mars- which was associated with war due to the fact that iron could conquer or overcome other metals).

The next stage in the process is outlined by the FC penalty, where the 'heart and vitals are placed on the highest pinnacle of the temple, there to be devoured by the vultures of the air". This alludes to the distillation stage in alchemy where the vital oils and essence of the herb rise up to the highest point of the distillation apparatus as air, only later to fall again (or condense) like dew into another flask. This process actually divides the herb- leaving the body of the herb behind while separating the heart and vitals of the herb- or oils and spirits from the rest of the flask. In early alchemical texts, this stage was represented by vultures picking out the heart and other organs and taking them to the highest tower- which represented the top point of the athenor- or alchemical distillation apparatus. This athenor was often depicted in alchemical texts as a tower, since the apparatus looked like one. Something else happens at this stage as well, which relates to the FC degree penalty in some jurisdictions. As the liquids leave the remaining ground up herb, tiny holes start to form in the remaining ground up herb- which have the appearance of ground squirrel holes or prairie dog holes in a field. For those jurisdictions that have "beasts of the field" in their FC penalty- this is what it alludes to.

The next stage is in the MM degree, in which the penalty has the 'bowels burnt to ashes, and (t a s t t f w o h)". This alludes to the calcinations stage in alchemy of taking the herb (called feces at this stage due to it's digestion, and which naturally associates it with the bowels), and burning it to ashes by the action of fire and air (wind). This process is further emphasized by the password of this degree, who was the patron of metallurgy and fire from the Bible. Likewise, the strong grip of a MM is formed by placing the hand in the shape of the Hebrew letter shin- which in Hebrew qabbalistic tradition is equated with fire. This is why Hebrew priests also bless with their hand placed in this position, as do Eastern Orthodox priests.

Alchemists always revered Vulcan, also known as Tubelcain, as a patron of their art. From the 1530 alchemical writings of Paracelsus we read:

"Alchemy is a necessary, indispensable art... It is an art, and Vulcan is its artist. He who is a Vulcan has mastered this art; he who is not a Vulcan can make no headway in it. But to understand this art, one must above all know that God has created all things; and that He has created something out of nothing. This something is a seed, in which the purpose of its use and function is inherent from the beginning. And since all things have been created in an unfinished state, nothing is finished, but Vulcan must bring all things to their completion. Things are created and given to our hands, but not in the ultimate form that is proper to them. For example, wood grows by itself, but does not transform itself into charcoal. Similarly, clay does not become a pot. This is true of everything that grows in nature."

Now that the red ashes (called dead salts in alchemical terminology) have been created, they need to next be 'raised' or made alive. This is symbolic of the 'raising' of Hiram. The same motif is found in ancient Egyptian myth and ritual in which the body of the vegetation god Osiris had been cut up and symbolically killed and deposited in a tamarisk, and then when the goddess Isis turns herself into the lioness Sekmhet, she is able to raise him to new life). The raising of Hiram is done after the sprig of acacia, or evergreen is found, and it must be remembered that alchemical texts state that the 'spiritual' or 'alive salt' is found mostly in grapes, gold, and evergreen or pine. In alchemical texts, it is said that the "alive" salt is then turned into the Red Lion by the help of the sun and moon- as found on the rods of the JD and SD crossed over the raising. Finally, the "Red Lion", (which is another term for one aspect of the Philosopher's Stone: the other being "White Eagle"), is raised by the "lion's paw", and upon the (fpof). Some jurisdictions will recognize an "eagles claw" in place of the "lion's paw" and this is why. In alchemical language, the "fpof" was a term which alluded to the four elements with the addition of the fifth quintessence- or ether. It was symbolized by a blazing five pointed star- the same blazing five pointed star which is said to be found in the center of the checkered pavement- according to EA lecture. It is then that the 'word' of a MM, or Master Craftsman is spoken, and alludes to the Logos, or word of God spoken to he who has been prepared to hear it.

There are many theories surrounding the origin of the MM word. One theory about the origin of the MM's word is that it comes from the Hebrew "Manna Bon"- meaning: "what is it- the builder". We have already examined the alchemical association with manna and it's relation to the secret alchemical salt, which truly is the builder or cornerstone of the alchemical work. In fact, by using the Hebrew gematria, the word "manna" itself adds up to 90 (mem=40 and nun=50, which are the two letters in "manna" in Hebrew). This number, 90, also equals the number of degrees in a Master's square.

Another theory, is that comes from the ancient Egyptian "Ma-at Ben". "Ma-at"- pronounced as both "Mah-at" and "Maha" in ancient Egyptian, means "truth". The word "ben", on the other hand, means both "light" and "stone". This is why in ancient Egypt the phoenix was called the "ben-nu bird"- as it was associated with the alchemical process of consuming itself in flames and then coming back from the dead renewed. This word in Egyptian then, means both: "the truth of light" or the "truth of the stone"- both of which make perfect sense in the Masonic progression and to what the brother most desires at each degree. Interestingly, if we take the Egyptian word for "stone" and "light" and spell it backwards, we get the word "neb"- which was the Egyptian word for "gold". We see similar word play in the ancient Egyptian word for "brain"- "ais", which when reversed becomes "sia"- the ancient Egyptian word for "consciousness". This would suggest that elements of Masonic ritual have their roots in ancient Egyptian mystery tradition, which obviously most Masonic scholars are uncomfortable with accepting. However as outlined previously, there are many elements of Masonic ritual which we can find as fundamental components of ancient Egyptian practice and myth, even though Freemasonry went public almost 150 years before Egyptian Hieroglyphs were translated.

According to the historian Josephus, Moses was a high priest at Heliopis, called in ancient Egyptian "On", and this is in fact where the famed "ben-nu bird" was kept. It is perhaps coincidental that Solomon's name is composed of the word "sol", meaning sun, "om" another word which in Egyptian and Vedic scriptures was associated with the sun, and "on"- the Egyptian city associated with the sun, the phoenix (ben-nu bird), and thus later called by the Greeks "Heliopis"- meaning, "place of the sun". In fact, the Egyptian sun God RA was sometimes called "Omon" or "Amon", and this was later used to end Christian prayers with "Amen". The earliest prayers to Amon Ra began, "Amon- Amon who are in heaven, hallowed be thy name, thy kingdom come, thy will be done, on earth as it is in heaven," which was later used in the New Testament Gospel of Matthew (6:9-13 KJV). Of course, "Amon's" is also an anagram for "mason". Perhaps this is why the Regis Manuscript, being the earliest English manuscript that mentions the Masons, states that they came from Egypt. I will also point out that the sun in alchemical and Qabbalistic correspondence was associated with gold, and in both alchemical manuscripts and ancient Egyptian hieroglyphics, both the sun and gold were represented by a point within a circle- a familiar symbol to Masons.

One final interpretation of the MM Word is that it can be found within the Hebrew phrase "EBEN (MA)SU (HA)-(BON)IM"- meaning "the stone that the builders rejected". As mentioned previously, this related to the alchemical substance called "manna" or "secret salt". By more than coincidence, if we use the qabbalistic science of gematria and replace every Hebrew letter in this phrase with its numeric counterpart (as alluded to in the FC stair lecture), the phrase adds up to 273, which is also what "Hiram Abiff" adds up to in Hebrew using Gematria. All of this obviously very neatly ties back into the alchemical process we are describing.

The symbolic "hearing" of the MM's Word can be interpreted to represent the raised consciousness with the completion of the alchemical elixir. It is the trowel of the MM degree which is the tool that brings everything together, and represents the hidden force or fifth element which binds the various parts of the alchemically elixir-based stone. The elixir is made up of the Red Lion powder suspended in the 'dew', or oils and liquid saved from distillation. This also relates to the 133 Psalm, emphasized in the EA degree- 'the dew of Hermon...promising even life forevermore".

Finally, let us review the MM password: T:.. Again, this name is associated with being a metallurgist, or alchemist, (like Hiram) and master of the mineral kingdom. The password for the second degree alludes to the vegetable kingdom- as represented by the hanging corn. Corn- again, alluded to the salt in the alchemical process from which the body of the Philosopher's stone is made. In fact, vegetable alchemy was called the 'Lesser Work", and mineral alchemy (dealing with metals) was called the 'Greater Work' or sometimes the 'Great Art'. We should therefore not be surprised to learn that the password for the second degree has an alchemical allusion. In the FC degree ritual we are informed that the password for the second degree has "come to mean a sheaf of corn over a waterford"- but this does not mean that the actual translation of the word means this- nor does it mean that it always meant this. In fact, when we take the FC password and translate it into Greek, it spells σιβωλιθος : which translates as "I revere a stone". With everything else we have connected thus far, it is clear to see what kind of stone we are talking about- it is the alchemical stone, or Philosopher's stone.

On Hiram's tomb, as found in the Master Mason's lecture, we find further alchemical imagery. We see the figure of father Time, also associated with Saturn and by extension lead in alchemical imagery, counting the golden locks of the maiden- symbol of gold, as she stands over the urn of ashes and holds pine. If we accept this imagery literally, it makes no sense, as we are informed that Hiram was buried, and yet here we have a monument which shows the maiden weeping over his ashes- thus suggesting he was cremated. This is a contradiction unless we understand it as an alchemical allegory.

Some other traditional alchemical symbols in degrees are the chalk, charcoal and clay from the EA degree, which the chemist can use to make alkali and acid from in order to turn the reddish salts into the white 'alive salt'- called 'manna' in alchemical texts. With the charcoal we are also taught that "there is nothing more fervent than charcoal, to which, when properly ignited, the most obdurate metals yield." The point within a circle with two lines on either side was an old alchemical symbol of the amount of time it would take for gold to be made through the alchemical work; whereas just the point within the circle was the ancient symbol for the sun in nearly all cultures. In alchemical ciphers, the circle between two lines was a further symbol associated with what was said to be the symbolic alchemical year- or the time it takes to produce the Philosopher's Stone. The two lines on either side of the point within a circle, said to represent Saint John the Evangelist and Saint John the Baptist, may also allude to the believed alchemical tradition that Jesus inherited and passed on. Perhaps it should likewise not be surprising that the eagle was the traditional symbol for John, and a double headed eagle symbolized the two John's, and this was also the symbol for the "White Eagle" stage in alchemy. Albert Pike believed that the Scottish Rite inherited this symbol for this reason. It is therefore not coincidence that the feast day of John the Baptist, June 24th, was the former feast day of the Babylonian god Oannes- who was said to teach the alchemical science to civilization after he anointed priest kings and made them don aprons. Oannes later became Johannes, which in English became "John".

All of the emblems of the MM degree are from old alchemical manuscripts, most particularly the beehive. In alchemical symbolism, the beehive represented the lab (or lodge), where the bees (Masons) bring raw materials they have collected from the earth in order to transmute them into golden honey (lead into gold). The five pointed star in the center of the lodge was always an alchemical symbol for quintessence, as previously discussed, by which Sulphur, Salt, and

Mercury (symbolized by the tapers?) are turned into the Philosopher's Stone. This was further achieved with the help of the sun, moon, and alchemist- or "sun, moon, and Master of the Lodge", as in EA degree proficiency.

This correlation is particularly emphasized in the alchemical writing known as the "Emerald Tablet of Hermes", in which it says of the Philosopher's Stone that, "it's father is the sun, it's mother is the moon" (see Appendix A). Some have even seen the name "Hiram" as a Hebrew version of the name "Hermes"- who is credited with writing the alchemical text itself. (When you take the letters that spell "Hiram" in Hebrew and emphasize a different set of vowels- since Hebrew has no vowels, then it can be pronounced "Herme"- which is the Greek Hermes). Coincidently, the word "Herme" in Greek also means "pillar", and atop the Masonic pillars are the two globes. In Hermes' Emerald Tablet he says, "as above so, below; as below, so above" in order to produce the Philosopher's Stone. On the Masonic pillars are emphasized the "above" and "below" that Hermes speaks of. The Greek Hermes was the Roman Mercury- who was the messenger with a rod that had two snakes winding up it. This is why in some Masonic jurisdictions the Junior and Senior Deacons have Mercury- or Hermes on top of their rods. In other jurisdictions, the sun and moon are featured, which come directly from Hermes' Emerald Tablet. Again, from a qabbalistic standpoint, in the early alchemical diagrams of the qabbalistic tree (Jacob's Ladder), the middle pillar featured the sun, moon, and mercury- which would be the sun, moon, and Hiram- or sun, moon, and Master of the Lodge, represented by the burning tapers.

The Philosopher's Stone itself was always symbolized by a perfect cubic stone, which is a familiar symbol in the symbolic lodge of Masonry, and this "stone" is emphasized in the FC pass and MM word, as we pointed out. The other symbol it was sometimes depicted as was a circle, square, and triangle interlaced. This represented the spiritual gold circle, the four cornered square of the four elements, and the triangle of sulphur, salt, and mercury. In the center of every Masonic Lodge can be found a circle, square, and triangle- represented by the compasses, square, and three lesser lights. The 47th problem of Euclid, as credited to Pythagoras, was also a significant symbol to alchemists. This is because alchemists believed that it revealed the correct proportions of salt, sulphur, and mercury that needed to go into making the perfect elixir.

One of the remaining symbols of alchemy that is also significant to Masons was the Ark of Noah. To the alchemists, the myth associated with Noah related to the alchemical process itself. In the myth, the world is obsessed with material senses, representing earth; then a flood comes, representing water and the digestion stage; after which Noah lets a dove go into the air, representing the air itself and distillation; and finally Noah lands on Mount Ararat and makes a burnt offering to God, representing fire and calcination. Not surprisingly, the word "Ararat" in Sanskrit means "Illumined one". Many Sanskrit words crossed over into the Bible, but few readers of the Bible would recognize them. Another example is the word "Nazorean"- which is usually interpreted by Biblical readers as "watcher". However, in Sanskrit, the "Nazor" was the name of the third eye said to be opened at illumination. A "Nazorean" is then one whose third eye would be open, which may, in fact allude to the "eye of Deity" featured in the MM degree. Obviously this also alludes to Jesus the Nazorean- which is usually incorrectly interpreted as "Jesus of Nazareth" from the Greek. This third eye related to the pineal gland, situated right above and between the two eyes, which is in charge of regulating the glands of the autonomic nervous system. It also looks like a small pine cone- which is where it gets its name from.

Finally, as was shown in the alchemical process, the entire work went through nine stages composed of the substance turning black, red and white three times. Therefore it went through three times three changes, which should be significant to some Masons in relating to the Grand Honors of Masonry.

As can be seen from this Chapter, most of the Masonic symbols of the symbolic degrees can be found in older alchemical texts and allude to alchemical stages and processes. This is not to say that everything in Freemasonry has alchemical roots and meaning, but it is suggesting that if you really want to understand the Masonic symbols in the symbolic blue lodge degrees, then you have to have an alchemical understanding of what is behind them. This aspect of the craft was understood by Masons in the 1700's and even some, like Albert Pike understood that there was some kind of correlation in the 1800's. The complete meaning behind all of it may have even been lost to him however. There are more symbols that relate to the alchemical process in both the York and Scottish Rite, so therefore it is important that we examine these at least to a degree, in our next chapter.

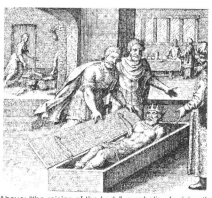

Above: "the raising of the body", symbolic of raising the stone to a new state in alchemy. M. Maier, Atlanta Fugiens, 1618.

Above: Herb being "raised" after essences have been extracted. This is done between the sun, moon, and Master figures. Aquinas, De Alchimia, 1526.
Below: Raised body- J. Lacinius, 1714.

Above: Raising the stone by the "lion's paw" until it is the Red Lion (which is another name for the Philosopher's Stone". M. Maier, Atalanta Fugiens, 1618.

Below: Symbol for the Philosopher's Stone: the squared circle. 1624.

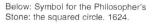

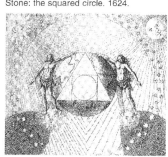

Below: Alchemical Cypher key of Valentinus- 1659. Notice how the symbols associated with "crucible" include a shape similar to the Master Mason's apron- as well as a Templar cross and skull and crossed bones.

Above:Noah's Ark in a alchemical plate from 1677. The opening of the work is compared by alchemists to the Biblical flood, as well as the rough sands of the sea.

Above: The vultures of the air taking the heart and vitals of an herb. D. Stolcius von Stolcenberg, Viridarium Chymicum- 1624.

Above- another plate showing the vultures of the air taking the vitals to the highest pinacle. M. Maier, Atlanta Fugiens, 1618.

Above: Bowels being removed (in this case eaten by a symbolic wolf), and then burnt to ashes. M. Maier, Atlanta Fugiens, 1618.

Left: Eye of Diety symbolizing the perfection of the alchemical art both on the above and below. Also featured in it is the sun, the earth, the moon, and a flaming sword- which was traditionally the symbol of a comet. J. Bohme, Theosophische Werke, 1682.
Below: "Use the rose to collect the honey". Here the bee and the bee hive is emphasized by Fludd in the alchemical work . Robert Fludd, Summum Bonum 1629.

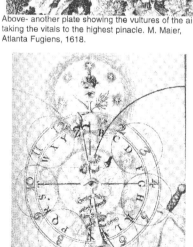

Above:(Top)This symbol was an alchemical symbol meaning 'year'. The symbol below it symbolized both 'gold' and the sun. The composite of these two is the familiar Masonic symbol.

Below: Alchemical plate from Albertus Magnus' Philophia Naturalis, 1650. Notice the compass in the upper right corner, the square and rule in the bottom right corner, the pot of manna in the lower left corner, the scales in the upper left corner, and then the figure's body is made up of the elements and he is surrounded by the sun and moon. Also on the top is the 'caput mortum' or 'dead head.'

Above: Alchemical plate of Anton Kircher, 1665. Notice the eye of deity. Also, one angel is holding a plumb, one a square, and one man holds a compass. The other man holds a Bible with a six pointed star and five pointed star on it. The six pointed star is what the Masonic emblem makes, and the five pointed star is on the checkered floor of the lodge. Finally, the 3,4,5 traingle of Pythagoras is shown- which is also found in the Master Mason degree. As stated in the paper, the 47th problem of Euclid was used by alchemists as a measure for how the three components of salt, sulpher, and mercury went together.

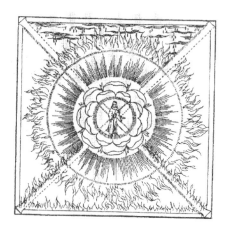

Putrefactio.

Resurrectio.

Top Left: Notice the Man making the duegaurd of a Master Mason, while being in the middle of a rose, cross, and the four elements. Taken from Secret Symbols of the Rosicrucians: 16th century.

Above: "The Philosopher's Stone" by Basilius Valentinus' Les Douze Clefs de la philosophie, 1659. Notice the perfect cubic stone, and how the king holds a compass. The lillies and roses allude to the white and red phase of the work. The sun and moon are further emphasized.

Above Left: Plates showing the 'caput morten' or 'dead head' stage, and also the 'resurrection' stage-associated with "raising" in the MM Degree. Taken from Secret Symbols of the Rosicrucians: 16th century.

Left: Alchemical diagram of Robert Fludd's showing the three divisions of man as in Masonic ritual, and how they allude to fire, air, and water. Above the man's head is the three pointed triangle of Light. Taken from Ultriusque Cosmi, Vol. II, 1619.

Right: The main portal of the Cathedral Notre Dame in Paris showing one of the many reliefs featuring alchemical symbolism. The woman (representing alchemy) has her head in the heavens and feet on the earth. The ladder is the steps in alchemy.

Chapter 4: The Upper Degrees

Both the Scottish and York Rites of Freemasonry continue with further instruction on the alchemical process. For example, the Scottish Rite brother who achieves the 32nd degree in the southern jurisdiction receives a black hat- symbolic of the black stage of the work. If he receives the honor of receiving the KCCH, then he receives a red hat- alluding to the red phase of the alchemical work. If he then receives the high honor of receiving the 33rd degree, he will obtain a white hat- representing the last alchemical stage in the process. The association with black, red and white in alchemy and the Scottish Rite degrees is mentioned in the degrees themselves, and many of the degrees- like the 27th degree (Knight of the Sun or Prince Adept), go into great detail about alchemy itself. These degrees make it clear that there are alchemical symbols in the degrees of Freemasonry if you can learn to see them. Perhaps this is also why symbols like the phoenix, raven, double headed eagle and pelican are found within the Scottish Rite- and all allude to alchemical processes in the creation of the Philosopher's Stone in alchemical texts.

Let's look at the apron of the 18th degree (Knight Rose Croix), for example. On it is found a pelican pecking it's own breast to feed it's young with a cross coming out behind it surmounted by a rose. In the middle ages, and alchemical vessel was actually called a pelican, and the components in it were symbolically said to destroy itself in order to give birth to it's new, young form. The cross was a symbol of a crucible, which is why crucifix and crucible have the same root. The rose not only represented the unfolding of consciousness out of the cross of matter, but the word "ros" (a play on rose), is the Greek word for "dew". The word Rosicrucias- or "ros-i-crucias" therefore was a play on words for "dew chalice"- alluding to the alchemical work and the Holy Grail by extension. This degree makes further exploration of Hermeticism and alchemy if the lecture is closely listened to, and it will be heard that the Emerald Tablet of Hermes is quoted. Traditionally, in the Scottish Rite, when a brother attained the 18th degree they were entitled to place a symbol next to their signature, which consisted of a cross atop a triangle, which is a symbol from alchemy and it represents "the completion of the great work."

Albert Pike certainly explores alchemy a great deal in *Morals and Dogma*, as well as other works like his *Esoterika*, and he even suggests he at least has some understanding of certain aspects of the work. For example, on pg 780 of his chapter on "Knight of the Sun" or Prince Adept in *Morals and Dogma*, Pike says:

"The secret knowledge of the Grand Scottish Master relates to the combination and transmutation of different substances; whereof that you may obtain a clear idea and proper understanding, you are to know that all matter and all material substances are composed of combinations of three several substances, extracted from four elements, which three substances in combination are salt, sulphur, and spirit. The first of these produces solidity, the second softness, and the third spiritual, vaporous particles. These three compound substances work potently together; and therein consists the true process for the transmutation of metals."

The Royal Arch and Cryptic Mason degrees of the York Rite delve quite a deal into the "key-stone" of Hiram, which is white "because white is the color of manna." In fact manna is a critical aspect to these degrees, and it is always related to the "stone that the builders rejected"; a term which is fundamental to the alchemical terminology for manna- or the secret white salts, which are to be found everywhere, but no one but the alchemist knows how to see and raise them. In the York Rite the title "Thrice Illustrious" is used, which was the title for the Greek god Hermes- said to be the inventor of alchemy and the author of the Emerald Tablet. Manna is also emphasized with Aaron's rod- both of which go into the Ark. In early York Rite rituals, Aaron's rod was depicted as a rod with two snakes entwined around it, which was the wand of Hermes. One snake was red and one was white- representing the red and white aspects of the Philosopher's Stone, among other things. The Royal Arch "gates" and banners are likewise composed of all of the colors that the Philosopher's Stone itself can become- blue, red, purple, and white, all of which were used to create some of the colors in the stained glass of the cathedrals of Notre Dame.

In both the Scottish Rite and the York Rite one symbol that is always featured is the Seal of Solomon, or the six pointed star- also called the Star of David. This symbol is composed of two interlaced triangles, and some have suggested that this is also what the square and compasses make when they are interlaced. What is significant from an alchemical standpoint is that in ancient alchemical symbolism, fire was represented by an upward triangle, air by an upward triangle with a line through it, water with a downward triangle, and earth with a downward triangle with a line through it. If you combine all of these together into one composite symbol, the end result is the Seal of Solomon. This symbol then, from an alchemical standpoint, represented the combination of all the elements into one whole, and by extension represented the Philosopher's Stone itself. Perhaps not surprising to Masonic historians is the fact that first place this symbol showed up on monuments in Europe was not at Jewish temples, as would be assumed, but rather in temples designed and built by the Knights Templar.

There are hundreds of more alchemical symbols in both the rites, too many to mention them all here in this book. However it must be added that both Rites delve into the significance of the Knights Templar, which are pivotal in alchemical history. There are two prevailing schools of thought as to where Freemasonry came from: one is that it came directly from the Knights Templar after their suppression in 1307, and the other is that it came from the cathedral builders of the Middle Ages. However, we now know that it was the Knights Templar who provided the initial imputes for the cathedrals, as they created over 1,000 gothic style churches, cathedrals, and chapels in their short 200 years of public existence. These cathedrals, like Notre Dame of Paris, are completely covered with symbols showing the entire alchemical process. In fact, the front façade of Notre Dame of Paris has several images all along it which don't depict the Bible at all, but rather every stage in alchemy. Figures like the elusive St. Dennis is featured with his head cut off- symbolizing the caput mortum stage. St. Denis was actually the initiate Dionysus the Aeropagite- who was initiated in the Pythagorean alchemical schools which re-enacted the initiation rites of Dionysus- who was Osiris in Egypt. The same can be said of the other cathedrals- most particularly Chartres, which also features images of Knights Templar themselves, not to mention the Prophet Melchizadek holding a Grail chalice with the Philosopher's Stone in it, the point within a circle, and certain monuments that only light up inside the cathedral on St. John's day- June 24th . Chartres also features an alchemical clock sun dial, which shows which planet is ruling each hour of the day for alchemical operations.

So whether we are looking at cathedral builders or Orders of Knighthood as Freemasonry's origins, both theories lead to the same source- the Knights Templar. Since we also find alchemical symbols found in the actual old Templar Preceptories and churches, and since we know they were in contact with custodians of alchemy in the Holy Land- like the Sufi, then it is clear where this tradition came from. We should also not be surprised that it was the Knights Templar who invented CPR and used mould extracts for healing as a form of early alchemical experimenting with antibiotics. The Templars must have inherited alchemical texts, and along with possible archeological finds at the ruins of Solomon's Temple, were able to start to develop the science. Masonic bodies like the Royal Order of Scotland certainly suggest this Templar connection, and perhaps this is why the second degree password, when converted to the Greek σιβωλιθος, has a gematria value of 1307- which is the year of the Templar round up and persecution. Certainly the alchemists of the 1600's wrote fondly of the Templars, and these same alchemists published the first diagrams of "Masonic symbols" centuries before the craft announced itself to the public in 1717. It is also on the early Templar gravestones of Scotland that we find squares, compasses, a grail chalice, and the skull and crossbones- all of which later became associated with Freemasonry. The skull and crossbones, for example, related to the "dead head" or "caput mortum" stage of the work. These same skull and crossbones can be found painted in some old Templar buildings. The Templars also used the symbol of the rose-cross in their temples- later associated with the Rosicrucians.

Other Masonic bodies like the Allied Masonic Degrees, and the Masonic Societas Rosicruciana likewise contain alchemical symbols and instruction. Groups like the Masonic Societas Rosicruciana for example, contain blatant alchemical teachings in all of their degrees, which are not even veiled. These groups are by invitation only, so there are few Masons who are fortunate enough to experience and learn from their instruction. An interest in the alchemical aspects of Masonry certainly opens a brother up for consideration however!

Alchemy must therefore continue to stand as a cornerstone in the various Rites of Masonry. Again, by a greater understanding of the art, a greater understanding of the symbolic ritual and teachings of all these other aspects of Freemasonry can be understood. We have now examined how alchemy is related to Freemasonry, and we have also examined how it relates to chemical operations, but how does it relate to the initiation process of transmuting the individual? To answer this question, we must next look at the ancient initiation rites of the ancient world and see how they relate both to the alchemical process and to Freemasonry in particular.

TINCTURA

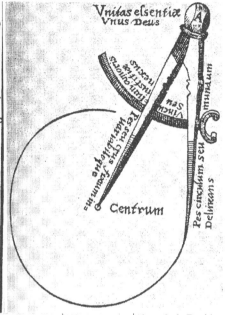

Unitas essentiæ
Unus Deus

Centrum

Fasciculus Chemicus:
OR
Chymical Collections.

EXPRESSING

The Ingress, Progress, and Egress,
of the Secret Hermetick Science,
out of the choisest and most
Famous Authors.

Collected and digested in such an
order, that it may prove to the advantage,
not onely of the Beginners, but Proficients
of this high Art, by none hither-
to disposed in this Method.

Whereunto is added, The Arcanum or
Grand Secret of Hermetick Philosophy.

Both made English

By James Hasolle, Esquire,

Qui est Mercuriophilus Anglicus.

London, Printed by J. Flesher for Richard Mynne,
at the sign of St. Paul in Little Britain. 1650.

Above Left: Double Headed Eagle from 16th century Rosicrucian Alchemical text.

Above Right: Compass diagram from Robert Fludd's Alchemical writings:1621.

Left: Chymical Collections of 1650- notice all of the Masonic emblems in the left hand pillar, with the sun and moon featured above, and the Master Hermes centered- who some associate with Hiram Abiff.

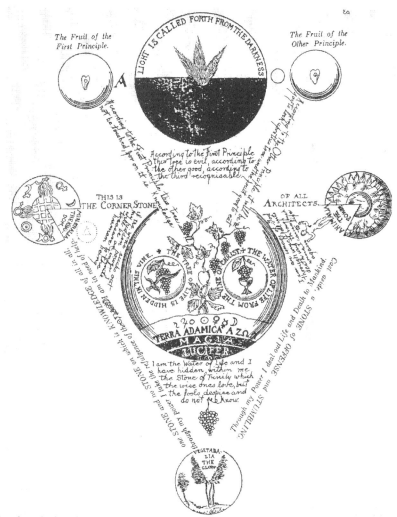

From Secret Symbols of the Rosicrucians, 16th century, this paticular plate is filled with Masonic symbolism. It starts out by showing how "Light is called forth from the darkness", and then shows the three kingdoms of mineral, vegitable, and animal. It also equates the "philosopher's stone" with the "corner stone of all architects," also the pine tree is shown, and in two places the point within a circle as a symbol for gold is shown.

Chapter 5: The Initiation Process

Fundamental to initiation processes like Freemasonry are the use of the four elements as found in the alchemical process. The alchemical process of an element always goes from earth to water (with digestion), from water to air (with distillation), and from air to fire (with calcinations). Likewise, the same use of elements was found in the ancient initiation schools of ancient Egypt, and later in the early Gnostic schools of Christianity, in which an initiate went through various "baptisms" by water, air, and fire at different degrees, or levels of study. This is very much like how Freemasonry emphasized water in the first degree, air in the second, and fire in the third degree.

Let me explain what the word "Gnostic" means, therefore, so we can understand it in context to Freemasonry. Gnosticism is the idea of the "Gnosis" or direct knowledge of the divine. The word "Gnosis" is the Greek word for "Divine Knowledge", and the Gnostics are mentioned many times in the Scottish Rite degrees. To the early Pagan Gnostics and later the early Christians- who were unquestionably Gnostic (if the scriptures are understood in the proper light), this Gnosis was something that was achieved through various stages of initiations and personal revelations. Fundamental to the idea of Gnosticism and by extension Christianity in its original form (and later Freemasonry) was the idea that All is God, but we are incarnated in a body which is like a tomb or a prison. Until we achieve consciousness breakthrough, we are living in our own personal Hell, of our own creating. After consciousness breakthrough, we come to the understanding that the kingdom of Heaven is all around us, but we just needed to open our eyes. The moment of awakening was called "Gnosis" and the center of the mystery was the Christos- or Christ in Christian traditions and Osiris in Egyptian traditions. In this capacity, Christ does not need to be a person per se, but rather a state of consciousness that is achieved when the crown of the head becomes awakened. The initial physical feeling of such an experience is usually accompanied with the feeling like oil is being poured all over your head- which is in fact the origin of the word "Christos"- meaning "anointed one". This may even have some relation to the excretion of certain hormones from the pineal and pituitary glands in the head- which are associated with the crown and 'third eye' (mentioned previously). "Christos" is the Greek word for the Hebrew "Messiah"- both of which mean "anointed". The ritual of anointing Kings on the head can be found going back to ancient Egypt and Sumer and is alluded to throughout the Bible- for example in Psalm 133:

"Behold! How good and how pleasant it is for brethren to dwell together as One. It is like the precious anointment upon the crown that ran down upon the beard- even Aaron 's beard, which ran down to the skirts of his garments. As the dew of Hermon, and as the dew that descended upon the mountains of Sion, for there the Lord commanded the blessing of eternal life."

When we use the word "Gnosis" in the western tradition, it is imperative that we do not make the mistake of thinking it is exclusively western and attainable only as Christians. In fact, words from other cultures refer to the same state. For example, individuals who have attained Gnosis are referred to as "Knowers" in Pagan, Taoist, and Christian traditions, "Arifs" in Islam, "Gnanis" in Hinduism, "Buddhas" or "Bodhisattvas" in Buddhism, and we also see the idea in words like "enlightened" or "Illuminated". This is why Freemasonry accepts brothers of all faiths who have a belief in God, and it is not the responsibility of Freemasonry to tell a brother what religion to follow.

As Freemasons, we need to be principally concerned with the Christian drama however, and the symbolism associated with it, as it relates also the symbolism found in the Masonic degrees themselves, and to the meanings behind the experiences associated with Hiram. Therefore we will examine the path to Gnosis from this early Christian vantage point. Keep in mind that this same myth can be found in different forms all over the ancient world- including with Mithras, Krishna, Odin, Buddha, Jupiter, Apollo, Dionysus, Indra, Pythagoras, Semiramis, Prometheus, and even Quetzalcoatl. This being the case, even though we are looking at the Christian myth, keep in mind that the initiation aspects of this myth are actually universal.

Within the Gnostic tradition, there were four states of consciousness with three initiatory steps between them. The first type of personality was represented by earth and involved people whose consciousness were totally obsessed with the physical world, the physical senses and by extension their own ego. These personalities were referred to as "Hylics", and the early Christians taught that they identified with a false physical body- called the "eidolon"- or double. Biblical terminology referred to these people as "blind" or "dead" or "asleep", since they couldn't perceive the spiritual root of things and didn't understand that their true body was spiritual and not physical. Since they were consumed with their ego, this ego was sometimes represented symbolically by a donkey- since the animal can be so stubborn. Overcoming this stage was usually represented by the person riding the donkey- symbolizing control over the lower nature- and represented by Jesus riding into Jerusalem on a donkey, or other Avatars like Mithras and Osiris also riding the donkey in their traditions. In the story of Pinocchio, he almost turns into a donkey when he is obsessed with his own ego, but later turns into a real boy when he overcomes this stage of development. Restoring Hylics to the spiritual path was therefore alluded to as "giving the blind sight" or "raising the dead". Throughout the Bible, places of slavery or bondage usually represented this hylic state- for example the earth before the flood, the slavery of Egypt, or the control of Rome being a few examples. Again, this stage was associated with the "earth bound" personality of the alchemical elements.

Once a person had an experience of the divine nature of the world however, they underwent a change of heart, so to speak. Most English translations of the Bible refer to this change of heart as "repentance"- though the Greek word associated with it is "metanoia." "Metanoia" didn't mean that you need to confess to a Priest or join a church, or apologize to God for "missing the mark"- as it is so often interpreted, but rather that you simply changed your heart and your focus towards attempting to understand your connection with God, and you were therefore free in the truest sense. It is the first step in spiritual awakening, and in Freemasonry it is symbolized by the sharp implement being pressed against the heart at the EA degree. This stage of initial awakening symbolically was represented as the realization that you live in a prison of your mind or in a tomb and the first initiation usually involved baptism by water- sometimes referred to as a "catharmos" or purification in early texts. This water stage represented the soaking of the herb in a vessel in the alchemical process. Some Masonic traditions to this day still start the first degree with the candidate starting out in a small dark room which has bread and water- like a prison, as well as symbols pointing to the way out of that prison. The initiation then proceeds with the candidate's first initiation out of the symbolic prison- which makes the brother a free-Mason, and thereby freeborn, and of their own free will and accord. The first stage of initiation was generally concerned with ethics. It was called the "psychic" stage by early Gnostics, and it was a stage in which the initiate discovered they were not merely a physical body.

The next initiation was usually done with air or breath and was called "pneumatic" and alluded to the distillation stage in alchemy. A pneumatic initiate came to understand their nature in impersonal terms and God not as a person on a cloud somewhere, but rather as the One. Duality begins to become transcended and all relationships with God begin to be brought into Oneness. God and the initiate become the mystery of God in love with itself. All is perfectly One. In the ancient Gnostic mystery theatres of Egypt, the various parts of the body of the slain Osiris represented different aspects of reality that all had their roots in this One source. The parts of Osiris are recollected and put back together through the love of Isis. The pneumatic initiate came to understand that if God was a point within a circle, and the outer circumference of the circle represented the physical form, then lines of radius emanating from the point in the center of the circle represented various stages of consciousness and various personas of the One. In the outer circumference of the circle each radius appeared as unique and distinct, but at the source of all was God- the mystery of mysteries. This is why the word "God" comes from the Hebrew letter "Yod", which symbolized a point. The point within the circle therefore not only represents gold and the sun, but part of the Gnostic initiation process. Getting to the center of the circle was the path of Gnosis, which is why Christ said that those who came before him were baptized with water and air, but he came to baptize with fire. Fire represented the initiation into Gnosis, and in alchemy, we associate it with the calcination stage.

The path from ignorance to Gnosis and the initiation of water, air, and fire was said to be symbolically illustrated throughout the Bible, as mentioned already with Noah. However even Moses' name is spelled Mem-Shin-Aleph- composed of the three Hebrew mother letters which are associated in the qabbala with water, fire, and air respectively. Moses' crossing of the Red Sea, his manna from heaven, and his witness of the burning bush all represent aspects of the elementary initiatory process. Let us also not forget that Moses dies in the desert, but Jesus Ben Nun led the people to the Promised Land- symbolizing Gnosis. The name "Jesus" or "Yeheshua" is spelled the same as the name of God "Yahweh" in Hebrew- only the Hebrew letter "shin" is inserted in the middle of the name. "Shin", it will be remembered, related to the MM strong grip and to fire.

At some point in the pneumatic process, attachment to the false self- or eidolon had to symbolically die so that the new higher spiritual body- sometimes called the "daemon" could awaken. This is why Moses had to symbolically die for Jesus Ben Nun to lead the people out of captivity and into the Promise Land. The word usually translated as "resurrection" in the Bible is the Greek word "anastasis", which actually means "awakening". This awakening was the Gnosis and the Christ. The Christ was the point within the circle that Gnostics were trying to reach, and it is symbolically why that point lies between the two Saint John's in Masonic EA instruction. This is why "doubting Thomas" questions Christ's awakening. "Thomas" means "twin" in Greek- and represented the eidolon- or false physical self. This is also how it came to be in Islam that the Koran suggests that someone other than Jesus died on the cross for Jesus. The Koran says, "They did not kill him. They did not crucify him. They were taken in by an appearance." Islamic Gnostics, such as Ishmaili Shiites and Sufi Sunnis teach that they represent the true Islamic tradition of which Mohammed and the original Muslims were initiated into. It was these same initiation groups that the Knights Templar had come in contact with and learned alchemy from. This tradition came from the Gnostic teachings and Apocryphal texts which suggested that the false twin- or eidolon symbolically died on the cross and Jesus awakened to the Christos of Gnosis. Mystery school tradition maintains that the tying of an initiate to a cross at this stage, or a symbolic death of some kind, goes all the way back to ancient Egypt. Like the original Christians, Islamic Gnostics treat Christ as an image of the consciousness of God, our shared essential identity. This was all symbolic, of course, to the initiatory and psychological path that we all take, and to the early Christians it was irrelevant if a man named Jesus actually went through this crucifixion or if he actually had a twin brother named Thomas. What mattered is that each Christian symbolically went through the symbolic death in order to realize

Christ, and by extension a reintegration with God and an understanding of the spiritual Kingdom all around them. This same symbolic death obviously occurs in the MM degree, as the brother represents Hiram Abiff. In alchemy, as was shown, it related to the death of the herb and then the raising of it to a new life. The death in the third degree occurs right after the third eye is whacked on the forehead- the place called the "nazor" in Sanskrit, and again related to the word "Nazorean". In ancient Egyptian, the word for the gods "neteru", actually meant the exact same thing as Nazorean, and it was sometimes represented by the eye of Osiris or the eye of Horus. This third eye must be opened for Gnosis to occur, which is why Jesus said "if thine eye can be single, they whole body will be full of light".

The symbolic death for a "third degree" can be found going back to ancient Egypt and Sumer as mentioned. In fact, some researchers suggest that the raising of Lazarus from the dead by Jesus was just such a reenactment of this ancient mystery school drama. The name "Lazarus" in Hebrew is "El Ausor". "El" was a Hebrew name for God, and "Ausor" was the Egyptian name for the God Osiris- who symbolically dies and was raised from the dead. In fact, in the Mandean Gnostic tradition of the Middle East, one of the names for God continues to be "Aursor", and they to this day refer to themselves as "sons of the widow". The early Gnostic Manichean sect likewise referred to themselves as "sons of the widow". The story of Lazarus takes place in Bethany, which in Hebrew is "Bethanu". "Beth" in Hebrew means "house" and "anu" in ancient Egyptian was the abode of the dead. Therefore "Bethany" or "Bethanu" means "house of the dead". Interestingly, if we change the Hebrew name for Lazarus around so that "El" is last and "ausor" is first, we get the name "Ausorel" or "Azrael"- which is the angel of death. In any event, it is widely believed by researchers that the raising of Lazarus was illustrating an initiatory rite, which is why Jesus took so long to go get him out of the cave he was symbolically buried in.

According to the Gnostics, Christ in the Bible and Osiris in the old world traditions represented the Consciousness of God, and his wife known as the Sophia in early Christianity- meaning "wisdom", and Isis in the Egyptian rites, represented individual psyche. Christ represented the point within the circle and Sophia represented the radius extending from the center to the outer circumference. One end of the radius is rooted to the center of Consciousness (Christ) and the other is tied to the body of the world. In this we see the gradations from the ether and fire down to the air, the water, and lastly the earth-represented by the objective world. The Sophia myth then reveals to us a story relating to a fallen goddess, attached to the physical (sometimes called "mortal Sophia"), who later through mystical marriage becomes united with psyche in a state of Gnosis- or united with Christ as the Universal or Enthroned Sophia. She represents the initiatory path that each Christian initiate takes, through the elements, and the marriage symbolizes the state of Gnosis that cannot be understood by those who have not attained it. The Gospel of Phillip states: "Bridegroom and bride belong to the bridal chamber. No one shall be able to see the bridegroom with the bride unless he becomes such a one." This is also why Paul challenges us to make Christ our husband. Even though many of the letters of Paul have recently been found to be later forgeries by the Roman Church, this helps to explain why Paul in some instances speaks strictly in Gnostic language and at other times condemns Gnosticism. The Roman Church used one of Christianity's greatest Gnostics and forged letters from him to be used to condemn Gnosticism- which was a rival movement to the literalist Roman Church of Constantine. This is why Paul tells us that he personally experienced Christ as a vision of light on the road to Damascus. "Damascus" was a code word used by the Essenes to refer to their base in Qumran, suggesting Paul has Essene affiliations. We find the same Damascus reference in the myth surrounding Father CRC in the Rosicrucian alchemical manifestoes of 1604 and1616, whose Chemical Wedding has the same mystical marriage allegory. This is also why Jesus transmutes water into wine at a wedding ceremony, and why we find wine later used again at the Last Supper. The Last Supper represents the point right before the Sophia is united with Christ and the false self dies. Just as water is transmuted into wine at the wedding ceremony, wine is turned into the blood of Christ at the Last Supper.

The early Christian Gnostics understood Mary Magdalene to symbolically represent Sophia- which is why Mary was the first to witness Christ after the awakening- or resurrection, and then proclaimed "the tomb is empty". This is also why she was symbolically said to have seven demons cast from her by Jesus-which represented the removing of the blockages of her seven psychic centers, and the awakening of the seven main glands that were associated with the seven planets, and by extension the seven liberal arts and sciences. This is also why Leonardo DaVinci painted her attached to Jesus at the Last supper, and Sophia has also been intimately linked with the Holy Grail. Let us not forget that the Gnostic doctrine of Sophia was utilized by Pagan Gnostics prior to the development of Christianity, and this is why the Pagan Gnostic Pythagoras coined the term "philosophy"- or "lover of wisdom"- "lover of Sophia", and this relates directly to our Philosopher's Stone. This is why we should not be surprised to find that Pythagoras is credited with miraculously catching 153 fishes, being immaculately conceived, raising the dead, and referring to himself as the son of God. (This account can be found in the writings of Porphyry and other early Pythagoreans). We also find the Sophia myth echoed in the story of Isis in ancient Egypt- who was the first to see Osiris rose from the dead just as Mary Magdalene was the first to see the risen Christ. This strongly suggests that early Christianity arose from the mingling and interaction of the Pythagorean Theraputae and the Jewish Essene mystery traditions- both of which had common origin in the Egyptian mystery schools, and both of whom have common origin in Freemasonry Blue Lodge instruction. The Scottish Rite degrees, like the Knight of the East and the West, likewise makes this association.

Since these symbolic initiation rites can be found both in Freemasonry and in the early Gnostic schools, then there has to be a connection. Since the same initiations with the alchemical elements follow the exact process for producing the Philosopher's Stone alchemically, then the initiations had to follow this alchemical process, and therefore the initiate was symbolically being transmuted to a greater form just as alchemy transmutes matter from a base to a precious form. The alchemical process is therefore not just about the production of chemical elements in the lab, but more importantly, this is the model for the production of a more enlightened person. By raising brothers in Freemasonry, we are likewise taking them through this initiation and alchemical process.

Chapter 6: Conclusion

In conclusion, I hope I have demonstrated that nearly all of the symbolism in Masonry, while at first glance appearing to be building symbols, are actually referring to the more hidden and esoteric craft of alchemy. While many symbols in Masonry also appear to relate to such subjects as sacred geometry and the qabbalah, both of these fields of study were also used and incorporated by the alchemists- as was the art of sacred architecture and leaving alchemical landmarks- or books in stone. Alchemy had already been a secret craft by the middle ages, but even at that time it was being outlawed by Kings and Popes, (even though a few kings and popes enslaved alchemists to fill their coffers). To the alchemist, his ability to do his craft made him more honorable than King, Prince, or Potentate, as he knew secrets of nature that these rulers did not; but this also made him highly resented and wanted. For this reason, if its knowledge was to be passed on, it needed to be incorporated in secret ritual that would be preserved from generation to generation. Freemasonry proved to be one of the greatest preservers of the alchemical secrets, symbolism, and practice, so that even today an avid student can recombine the entire process within the ritual. In this way, the light never dies out, and the moral responsibilities demanded in order to have the keys to the alchemical art are inculcated.

Many will argue that if the alchemical process of turning baser metals into gold was an actual possibility, then surely our modern science would have discovered it by now. However the historical record shows that A) transmutation has been proved many times over the centuries, and B) modern science, (which stemmed from alchemy), is only now with quantum physics and the atomic age starting to figure out that transmutation is a fundamental law of the Universe, and that what these modern physicists are writing now perfectly reflects what many alchemists wrote centuries ago. Modern science still has a way to go, and the people still need to become morally mature enough to handle it. In our modern age however, the process of turning baser metals into gold has been accomplished many different ways by scientists. Only Freemasonry and other traditional Orders have held the keys for transmutation to take place on all levels however- both externally, and within the initiate himself. This topic of the alchemical process appears to have been more common in lodges of the past, as evidenced by the works of Albert Pike and others who talk thoroughly of alchemy, but the subject has gradually been forgotten and not passed on to the brethren shortly after the time of the civil war in America.

This has left Freemasonry in America in particular with a whole body of symbols which are only half understood from their original context in our country. I have found, from personal testimony, visitations, and the writings of Masons in other countries, that the topic of alchemy is still discussed in tiled symbolic lodges in some countries- including in the United States. The bottom line is that most of the symbols in Freemasonry can be found in earlier alchemical texts and works, which makes it apparent that Freemasonry adopted this system sometime in the past. Understanding the context of these symbols, from their original source, helps us to gain a better understanding of their use in the rituals we continue to promulgate today within Freemasonry. This greater understanding, therefore, leads to Greater Light, and that is why I have written this book. I hope it has been illuminating and will empower you on your Masonic path.

Appendix A-

The Emerald Tablet of Hermes
(As Translated by Sir Isaac Newton c. 1680)

"Tis true without lying, certain & most true. That which is below is like that which is above & that which is above is like that which is below to do ye miracles of one only thing.

And as all things have been & arose from One by ye meditation of One: so all things have their birth from this One thing by adaptation.

The father is the sun, the moon its mother, the wind (air) hath carried it in its belly, the earth its nurse.

The father of all perfection on ye whole world is here, Its force or power is entire if it be converted to earth. Separate thou ye earth from ye fire, ye subtle from the gross sweetly and with great industry.

It ascends from ye earth to ye heaven & again it descends to ye earth and receives ye forces of things superior & inferior.

By this means you shall have ye glory of ye whole world & thereby all obscurity shall fly from you.

Its force is above all forces. For it vanquishes every subtle thing & penetrates every solid thing. So was ye world created.

From this are & do come admirable adaptations whereof ye means (or process) is here in this. Hence I am called Hermes Trismegistus (the thrice illustrious), having the three parts of ye philosophy of ye whole world.

That which I have said of ye operation of ye sun is accomplished & ended."

Selected Bibliography

Chevalier Emerys, *Revelation of the Holy Grail*, 978-0-6151-5878-5, lulu press, 2007.

Charpentier, *Louis, The Mysteries of Chartres Cathedral*, translated by Sir Ronald Fraser, RILKO Books, Athenaeum Press, Sussex, 2002.

Codex Rosae Crucis- DOMA: A Rare and Curious Manuscript of Rosicrucian Interest, introduction and commentary by Manly P. Hall, Philosophical Research Society, Los Angeles, 1938.

Franklin, Benjamin, *Wit and Wisdom from Poor Richard's Almanack*, The Modern Library, 2000.

Fulcanelli, *Le Mystere des Cathedrales*, translated by Mary Sworder, Brotherhood of Life Inc, 2000.

Fulcanelli, *The Dwellings of the Philosophers*, Archive Press, Boulder, Colorado, 1999.

Freke, Timothy and Peter Gandy, *Jesus and the Lost Goddess*, Three Rivers Press, New York, 2001

Hall, Manly Palmer, *Orders of the Great Work: Alchemy*, Philosophical Research Society, Los Angeles, 1949.

Hoyos, Arturo De, *Scottish Rite Ritual Monitor & Guide*, The Supreme Council, 33*, Southern Jurisdiction, Washington DC, 2007.

Macoy, Robert, General *History, Cyclopedia and Dictionary of Freemasonry*, Masonic Publishing Company, New York, 1870.

Official Ritual: *Heredom of Kilwinning and Rosy Cross*, Grand Lodge of the Royal Order of Scotland, Edinburgh, 1998.

Paracelsus, *Hermetic & Alchemical Writings of Paracelsus the Great*, translated by Arthur Edward Waite, The Alchemical Press, Washington, 1992.

Jung, Carl G., *Psychology and Alchemy*, Routledge & Kegan Paul, London, 1968.

Mackey, Albert Gallatin, *The History of Freemasonry*, Masonic History Company, New York, 1898.

Pike, Albert, *Morals and Dogma*, The Supreme Council of Southern Jurisdiction, Charleston, 1906.

Pike, Albert, *Esoterika: Symbolism of the Blue Degrees of Freemasonry*, Scottish Rite Research Society, Washington DC, 2005.

Roob, Alexander, *Alchemy & Mysticism*, Taschen, New York, 1997.

Secret Symbols of the Rosicrucians of the 16th and 17th Centuries, Diffusion Rosicucienne, Chateau d'Omonville, France, 1997.

The Chemical Wedding of Christian Rosenkreutz, translated by Joscelyn Godwin, Phanes Press, Grand Rapids, Michigan, 1991.

Tresner, Jim, with paintings by Robert White, *Vested In Glory, The Aprons, Cordons, Collars, Caps, and Jewels of the Degrees of the Ancient & Accepted Scottish Rite of Freemasonry*, the Scottish Rite Research Society, Washington DC, 2000.

White, Michael, *Isaac Newton, The Last Sorcerer*, Fourth Estate Limited, Great Britain, 1997.

.